KINGS OF JAZZ

Louis Armstrong

BY ALBERT J. McCARTHY

A Perpetua Book ∞

South Brunswick and New York
A.S. BARNES AND COMPANY, INC.

70-3926

CONTENTS

ACKNOWLEDGEMENTS

Acknowledgement is due to the following for permission to quote from their publications :

Peter Davies, Ltd   (*Just Jazz* 1);   *Jazz Review*

Maher Publications   (*Down Beat*);   *Record Changer*.

INTRODUCTION

The problem that confronts any writer who takes Louis Armstrong for a subject is basically one of knowing what to select from the mass of available data. Armstrong is not only the most famous jazz musician in the world; he is also the most written about. Faced with the requirements of producing a book of some twenty thousand words that would need to satisfy both the newcomer and the more fully informed, the question of the form to be adopted became a paramount one. It is obvious that there must be a great deal of recapitulation of information which is well enough known to the long-term jazz enthusiast, and no matter how adroit one may be in cloaking established fact in a new guise, such matters as birth dates, years of joining and leaving different orchestras, highlights of a career and the listing of outstanding records can really only be presented in one fashion. In addition, it would be a fool rather than a brave man who could presume that he were able to say anything startlingly new about Armstrong and his playing. The hundreds of articles that have reviewed the great trumpeter's career, his style, his influence and his records from almost every conceivable viewpoint leave little room for anyone to come up with a completely fresh approach. In view of this I have tended to veer towards safety by keeping the less specialist reader in mind throughout.

As already indicated, source material on Armstrong is considerable. Two books have been published under his name, the first of which, *Swing that Music*, appeared in the thirties. In retrospect it seems unlikely that much of this was actually contributed by Armstrong himself and many of the views certainly do not agree with what he has expressed since. Although it also shows signs of editorial influence, *Satchmo—My Life in New Orleans*, first published in the U.S.A. in 1954, seems reasonably authentic. It is the first of a projected series of volumes and only goes as far as Armstrong's trip to Chicago in 1922 to join King Oliver's band, but despite certain shortcomings it is a valuable documentation. As this book is readily available I have kept the section on the early days relatively short. To balance this brevity about the period prior to Armstrong's emergence as a performer of international renown I have dealt with more recent times in some detail. The reason for this is that there has been considerable controversy about Armstrong's current performances, particularly relating to his announcements and stage mannerisms. As several aspects of this matter touch on such subjects as the growth of the jazz audience as a whole and the relationship of the performer to his audience, I felt that a discussion of these points would have an interest beyond the point where they concern Armstrong himself.

To a considerable extent the development of Armstrong the artist is reflected in his recorded output. It was logical, therefore, to arrange the chapters in relationship to his records. This is made doubly necessary by the fact that there can hardly be any writer on jazz who was a witness of the events which took place during the early part of Armstrong's career. Quite by chance I had talked about certain aspects of the trumpeter's development during the thirties with some musicians who were in his bands. When their comments were not passed in private conversations, and where they are relevant, I have included them in the text.

A listing of some of the most important Armstrong records will be found at the end of this book. They are based on what is currently available at the time of writing.

ALBERT J. McCARTHY

I

1900-22 — THE EARLY DAYS

When, on New Year's Day in 1913, Louis Armstrong discharged a pistol which he had found at home, he little realized that the sequence of events which followed his action were to set him on the road to international fame. The immediate result was that he was arrested and sent to a reform school, but it was there that he received the first rudimentary training in music from one Captain Jones. Many years later he returned to that home as a celebrity and the bugle on which he first played is still preserved.

In his book *Satchmo—My Life in New Orleans* Armstrong gives a fascinating account of his early life. Because the book is generally available and is fairly well known I do not propose to devote a great deal of space to his early life, preferring to document later periods more fully. However, the picture that emerges from a reading of his autobiographical volume is an interesting one, and the sociologist as well as the jazz fan will find Armstrong's descriptions of New Orleans life worthy of study. He speaks of a society

3

strictly governed by racial and economic discrimination with each racial group living in some degree of independence of others. It was also a society in which violence was never far from the surface and Armstrong tells of cases of murder with a nonchalance that could only arise from acceptance of such doings as part of the normal routine of life. He speaks with great affection of an early parade drummer 'Black Benny', who was reputed to be one of the toughest men in the area, and it is with awe that he relates that Benny was the only Negro who would go alone through the Irish quarter. In view of the lurid accounts he gives of the toughness of many of his companions, the Irish must have been ferocious indeed if they could cause those worthies to hesitate before stepping into their territory!

The early years of the twentieth century—Armstrong was born on 4 July 1900—found New Orleans flourishing as one of the widest open cities in the United States. It was to have a run of another seventeen years before the famous red light district was to close down and it catered for vice on a lavish scale. The famous New Orleans' *Blue Book* set out the attractions of the 'mansions' in glowing terms, stressing the high quality of the entertainment to be found within them and the culture of the madames who were in charge. Whatever one's taste in off-beat entertainment it could be found, for the American belief that the consumer is always right found its expression in a rather unexpected fashion in the red light district! It has been suggested that much of the history of New Orleans

4

at this time has been romanticized and there may indeed be some truth in the criticism, but the guitarist Danny Barker has been gathering material for years on early New Orleans days, mainly from interviews with other musicians, and the parts of his manuscript that I have read would not suggest that much exaggeration would be needed to give a colourful picture of the era.

Armstrong accepted all that went on around him and was absorbed in the music he heard. He recalls listening to the legendary trumpeter Buddy Bolden, but says that he thought Bolden's playing was very rough. The parade bands fascinated him and he was first to take part in them as a member of the Waifs' Home band. However, his first musical experience in the form of actually entertaining others arose from his membership of a vocal quartet which included 'Kid Shots' Madison and 'Kid' Rena. This quartet used to wander around New Orleans singing in the streets for pennies. Its career was cut short when Louis was sent to the Waifs' Home.

In William Russell's article on Armstrong that appeared in the book *Jazzmen*, a story is related by Bunk Johnson which attempts to prove that Armstrong had played cornet before he was sent to the Waifs' Home. Johnson claimed:

'During that time (1911) Louis started after me to show him how to blow my cornet. When the band would not be playing I would have to let him carry it to please him.

'Now here is the time I began showing Louis. I took a job playing in a tonk for Dago Tony on Perdido and Franklin

5

Street and Louis used to slip in there and get on the music stand behind the piano. He would fool with my cornet every chance he could get until he could get a sound out of it. Then I showed him just how to hold it and place it to his mouth and he did so and it wasn't long before he began getting a good tone out of my horn.'

The difficulty with the *Jazzmen* article is that Russell was far too uncritical of Johnson's claims, and in his autobiography Armstrong includes a passage which is a flat contradiction of the above. It is worth quoting in full:

'The little brass band was very good, and Mr. Davis made the boys play a little of every kind of music. I had never tried to play cornet, but while listening to the band every day I remembered Joe Oliver, Bolden and Bunk Johnson. And I had an awful urge to learn the cornet. But Mr. Davis hated me. Furthermore I did not know how long they were going to keep me at the Home. The judge had condemned me for an indefinite period which meant that I would have to stay there until he set me free or until some important white person vouched for me and for my mother and father. That was my only chance of getting out of the Waifs' Home fast. So I had plenty of time to listen to the band and wish I could learn to play the cornet.'

It can be seen from this that Johnson's story was spurious. It is sometimes difficult to check information, but William Russell might have been a little more cautious in accepting a story which is at variance with claims made by Armstrong as early as 1935.

6

Armstrong was fourteen when he left the Home. He took a number of jobs during the day including that of coalman, milk roundsman and rag-and-bones man. He relates that his first job as a musician was obtained for him by one, Cocaine Buddy, and that it was in a honky tonk that catered for the good time girls when they were not working. Various jobs of this nature followed and around 1915 Armstrong formed his first band with drummer Joe Lindsey, patterned after 'Kid Ory's Brown Skinned Babies' in which King Oliver was the cornet player. In 1917 the band broke up and he again played with various groups which are now forgotten, but in the following year he got his first big break when Kid Ory called on him to replace Oliver who had left for Chicago. From now on Armstrong was a full time musician, for Ory had a tremendous local reputation and obtained most of the good jobs that were going. While he was with Ory, Armstrong also joined the famous Tuxedo Brass Band, led by Oscar 'Papa' Celestin. His fame spread amongst the New Orleans musicians of the day and he could more or less take any job that he wanted. It is a matter of regret that the recording of jazz had not been started a decade earlier, for one can only speculate on the nature of the music played in New Orleans during the formative years of jazz. Many musicians have claimed that Oliver was long past his prime by the time he recorded in 1923.

It was in 1918 that Fate Marable called on Louis and offered him a job in his band on the S.S. *Sidney*. His offer was accepted and the experience proved a valuable one for the young musician. Marable, in his time, had some of the greatest jazz musicians in his various bands, and he played a more varied selection of material than most of the New Orleans bands. It was a hard routine on the riverboats, as Armstrong recalled in *Swing that Music*:

'Hot musicians throw a pack of energy into their work, and it takes a lot out of them. When we ran those all-day excursions, and we did that at most all the ports we touched at, it only left about two hours to rest up and get dressed and ready for the evening excursions.'

The other members of the band when Armstrong joined were Joe Howard, David Jones, Boyd Atkins, Johnny St. Cyr, Baby Dodds, George 'Pops' Foster and Marable himself. David Jones, the mellophone player, was the first person who really taught Armstrong how to read music and he soon became proficient enough not to need to sit out when a new orchestration was produced until such time as he could memorize the number by ear. It would appear from the testimony of Fletcher Henderson which is quoted in the next chapter that Armstrong's reading abilities were not all that impressive at the time he joined the Henderson band, but at least he had some rudimentary knowledge of the subject by 1924. The life of a travelling musician seems to have appealed to Armstrong and he made several trips with Marable, finally leaving him for good in 1921. During one of the excursions he first met Bix Beiderbecke at Davenport, Iowa.

When he was not working on the boats Armstrong took various jobs in New Orleans. In 1921 he was playing at the famous Tom Anderson's cabaret on Rampart Street with a quartet led by a fiddler, Paul Dominguez. This was an extremely remunerative engagement with the musicians earning much more from tips than from any regular salary. When Anderson's closed down for repairs Armstrong worked in a trio with drummer Zutty Singleton and pianist Udell Wilson at a club owned by Butsy Fernandez. During the daytime there were the jobs with the Tuxedo Brass Band, and Armstrong has related his pleasure in being a member of that group in the following words:

'When I played with the Tuxedo Brass Band I felt just as proud as though I had been hired by John Philip Sousa or Arthur Pryor. It was a great thrill when they passed out the brass-band music on stiff cards that could be read as you walked along. I took great pains to play my part right and not miss a note. If I made a mistake I was brought down the whole day, but Celestin quickly saw how interested I was in my music. He appreciated that.'

In 1922 Armstrong was once more playing at Tom Anderson's in a group that included Albert Nicholas, Barney Bigard and Luis Russell. He was receiving frequent letters from King Oliver asking him to join his band in Chicago as second cornet player, and in the summer of that year decided that he would accept the invitation. He relates that he had become convinced that Oliver was the only person for whom he would leave New Orleans, having

9

witnessed too often the departure of other musicians with high hopes that were never to be fulfilled. He found the other members of the Tuxedo Brass Band anxious to dissuade him from leaving and they reported that Oliver was on the musicians' union's unfair list. This is a story that seems to have no basis in fact and was presumably an invention of those men who did not wish him to leave.

On 8 August 1922, Armstrong played at a funeral at Algiers in the afternoon. The funeral was for the father of Eddie Vincent, a trombone player of some local renown who later made a few records in Chicago. When it was over he went home, collected his clothes, and went to the Illinois Central Station to catch the 7 p.m. train to Chicago. The whole band and many friends and neighbours came to see him off. The musicians were glad that he was to have the opportunity of making a name for himself, but thought that he should have gone out on his own and not as the second cornet player to Oliver. Armstrong himself had no such qualms and the final sentence in his book, *Satchmo—My Life in New Orleans*, tells of his joy when he informed the porters on the train that he was going to Chicago 'to play with my idol, Papa Joe!' Although he was unaware of it his path to fame and international acclaim had begun.

2

1922-29 — THE EMERGENCE OF A JAZZ GIANT

Armstrong's arrival in Chicago has been described by him in the course of an article on Joe Oliver, characteristically titled 'Joe Oliver is still King', in the *Record Changer* of July–August 1950. The following are his own words on the subject:

'I'll never forget the night I joined the Oliver band. They were playing at the Lincoln Gardens, at 31st near Cottage Grove, an old, famous spot. They used to call it the Royal Gardens—that's where these blues came from. Then when Joe Oliver came up they changed the name to Lincoln Gardens, and it *still* jumped. Paul Whiteman, Louis Panico (they were fixtures in Chicago then), and all the cats from Friar's Inn used to come up there. Business was great. Well, I came up to Chicago then, and I didn't come in on the train that Joe was supposed to meet. So that makes me come in all by myself. I looked all around and I didn't see

11

anybody. I said: "Lord, what's going to happen now?", and I wondered if I should go right back on the next train. I was just a youngster from New Orleans, and I felt real lost in Chicago. But a redcap told me: "Why don't you get a cab and go out to the Lincoln Gardens?"

'When I got there and got out of the cab, I heard this band. They were really jumping then, and I commenced to worry all over again. I wondered if I could ever fit into that band. Oh, those cats were blowing! Old Johnny Dodds was making those variations and Baby Dodds shimmying on the drums. Dutrey was good on that trombone, too. He played shallow parts, which made them pretty, and he had a beautiful tone and punctuation. When I walked in that night I just sat down and listened.'

Armstrong's reputation had preceded his arrival, spread mainly by New Orleans musicians who had come up to Chicago. There is considerable disagreement concerning Oliver's relationship to his young admirer, some claiming that he had sent for him as a safeguard against his going with any other band and thus ending Oliver's own reign as 'king'. It has even been said that the Dodds brothers and Dutrey were enraged with Oliver for not allowing Louis to play lead, but it seems unlikely that they could seriously have expected the leader to take a subordinate role in his own band. Louis himself seems to have no such ideas and is always quick to praise Oliver, although he did say, in the previously quoted *Record Changer* article, that Oliver was already past his prime. Against the suggestions advanced

12

that Oliver was jealous of Louis must be laid the facts that he made him very welcome in Chicago, gradually allowed him to take more solos, and insisted that he studied music to fill in many gaps in his knowledge. The truth is probably that Oliver was well aware that Louis was the greater trumpeter and may have felt that he could do him less harm in his own band than with another leader, but that he also helped Armstrong to develop his talents is undeniable.

Whatever his failings might have been, the picture of Oliver that emerges from his series of tragic and moving letters that were printed in the book *Jazzmen*, is not that of a mean man. This view is supported on all sides, including the testimony of such an apparently unlikely witness as the late Lester Young who played with Oliver in his declining years.

The Oliver band acted as a catalyst on the development of jazz as a whole. The young men around Chicago who were becoming excited by the, to them, strange new music flocked to the Lincoln Gardens and in a very short while Armstrong's reputation had spread throughout the jazz world. There was little doubt in the minds of most of the listeners that Louis was the greatest member of the band and his acceptance as the most formidable soloist in the history of jazz dates from this period, although it was to be many years before he became known to the public at large.

On 31 March 1923 Armstrong entered the recording studio for the first time, as a member of the Oliver band.

13

The session took place in Richmond, Indiana, and the acoustical recording apparatus was very crude by today's standards. It is also said that the studio which the Gennett Recording Company used for these sessions was very close to a railroad track and that every time a train passed the session had to come to an abrupt halt. The fifth and last title recorded that day was *Chimes Blues*, and on this Armstrong took his initial recorded solo, of twenty-four bars length. During 1923 the Oliver band took part in a total of ten sessions for four different labels—Gennett, Columbia, Okeh and Paramount—and these sides have become classics of their kind. Actually, despite the presence of Armstrong and Johnny Dodds, the emphasis is on the ensemble sound of the group and solos are used quite sparingly. It may well be that Oliver was now past his best, but there can be little doubt that it was his firm leadership and awareness of the exact type of performance he wanted that made the records as great as they are. Musicians who heard the band in person swear that they give no real idea of how it sounded at the Lincoln Gardens and insist that the records are a travesty of the reality. In jazz there is a tendency for the older musician to romanticize about the past, but the extremely poor recording, coupled with the arbitrary three-minute time limitation of a ten-inch disc, obviously resulted in a great deal of the music being lost. One is only left to marvel that so much has come across in spite of these deterring factors.

The playing of the Oliver band is a supreme example

of the 'classic' New Orleans tradition. Since the nineteen-forties there have been dozens of attempts to emulate the band by young white 'revivalist' groups but none have come within measurable distance of its achievements. It is easy enough to point out that the musicians in the Oliver band were supreme of their kind, but this is only part of the story. For one thing, Oliver was particularly adept at selecting a tempo for the numbers played that did not strain the capabilities of his musicians. By comparison with the tempos chosen by many of the young white musicians who were influenced by the Oliver band, they seemed to be slower. It has been stated by fairly reliable witnesses that New Orleans musicians played blues at a much slower tempo in the early days than afterwards became fashionable and it is possible that this concept of tempo, presumably related to the needs of dancers, guided Oliver at the recording sessions. The beat of the band is even more important, for Oliver employed a straight four-four, whereas many of the revivalist rhythm sections have tended to accentuate the secondary beats. Perhaps the most impressive aspect of the Oliver records with Armstrong is the complete feeling of relaxation that comes across. There is none of the slightly uneasy feeling of effort that has become commonplace in the records of the revivalists: Oliver's music flows, or at least gives that impression, whereas the revivalists tend to sound jerky and this feeling destroys the effect of relaxation. This question has been well discussed by Larry Gushee, in a review of the Gennett

15

Oliver recordings, in *Jazz Review* of November 1958. What he says is so relevant to the matter that I am quoting part of his review:

'The truly phenomenal rhythmic momentum generated by Oliver is just as much dependent on *continuity* of rhythmic pulse—only reinforced by uniformity of accentuation in the rhythm section and relaxed playing. One never hears the vertiginous excitement of Bix, or Tesch; one never feels that, with a little less control, a break or an entire chorus would fall into irrationality or musical *bizarrerie*. Oliver's swing is exciting after a different fashion: it is predictable, positive, and consistent. Only rarely is the total effect *manqué*, as in *Froggie Moore*, where the stop-and-go character of the tune makes consistency more difficult to achieve.

'Its consistency is, as I have said, largely the result of Oliver's personal conception of a band sound. How much he moulded the musicians to fit the ideal pattern of his own imagination, or how much he chose them with the knowledge that they would fit in, without trying to change their personal style, is something we can't determine since we lack recordings by New Orleans bands before 1923.'

This discussion has more point than may at first appear, because the characteristics of much of Oliver's music in relationship to tempo, relaxation and rhythmic momentum are equally applicable to Armstrong's trumpet playing. Louis still speaks of this period as one of the happiest of his life and there is no stretching of credulity involved in

16

the suggestion that the disciplined music of the Oliver band was to teach him lessons that were to stand him in good stead in the following years.

The pianist with Oliver's band when he joined was Lil Hardin. Miss Hardin had received a classical training and her main interest at the time was still in the classical field. However, it did not take her long to perceive the inherent brilliance of Armstrong's playing and she helped him in his studies. In an essay on Armstrong in the book *Jazzmen*, William Russell states that by the time Louis had left the Oliver band his initial studies with Dave Jones and those with Lil Hardin had resulted in his becoming a proficient sight-reader. As we shall see later, Fletcher Henderson's testimony on the subject suggests that this is something of an exaggeration. What is certain is that, under Lil's guidance, Louis was assimilating a great deal more theoretical knowledge of music. Early in 1924 Lil Hardin and Louis were married and Lil did much to further his career in the next few years. In the summer of 1924 she managed to persuade Louis to leave Oliver and to take a job at the Dreamland Café as first cornet. Her motives for doing this were probably a mixture of pique at what she considered to be Oliver's reluctance to feature Louis enough and a genuine desire for his success as an individual performer. In September of that year Louis recieved a telegram offering him a job in Fletcher Henderson's orchestra and he left for New York City to take up the offer.

Fletcher Henderson's orchestra at this time was a vastly

different proposition from Oliver's. The *Chicago Defender*, the leading Negro newspaper in the U.S.A., said of Henderson's group that it was '. . . the greatest, not at all like the average Negro orchestra, but in a class with the good white orchestras, such as Paul Whiteman, Paul Ash, and Ted Lewis.' Of its music, it claimed that it was 'soft, sweet, and perfect, not the sloppy New Orleans hokum, but peppy blue syncopation.' This attitude on the part of the Negro press to authentic jazz is not as uncommon as might be assumed, and a whole book could be devoted to the subject. Certain aspects of the matter will be touched on in the last chapter. However, it is clear enough from the above that it was more a popular dance orchestra at this time (the great period of the band, when it was packed with outstanding jazz musicians, was to come a year or two later) than a jazz group, and Louis found it very strange at first. That he was a success from the start is attested by the late Fletcher Henderson himself who, writing in the *Record Changer* of July–August 1950, said:

'Needless to say, Louis was a big success right from the start. About three weeks after he joined us, he asked me if he could sing a number. I know I wondered what he could possibly do with that big fish horn voice of his, but finally I told him to try it. He was great. The band loved it, and the crowd just ate it up. I believe that was the first time he ever sang anywhere. He didn't sing with Oliver, I'm sure.

18

'The band gained a lot from Louis, and he gained a lot from us. By that I mean that he *really* learned to read in my band, and to read in just about every key. Although it's common today, it wasn't usual at that time to write in such keys as E natural, or D natural, so that Louis had to learn, and did learn, much more about his own horn than he knew before he joined us.

'That's how we influenced him. But he influenced the band greatly, too, by making the men really swing-conscious with that New Orleans style of his. The same kind of effect that Coleman Hawkins had on the reeds, that right-down-to-earth swing, with punch and bounce. He surely was an asset to my orchestra; I have no hesitation at all in saying that.'

Listening to the records that Armstrong made with the Henderson orchestra during 1924–25 one is amazed by the freshness of his solos even after an interval of over thirty years. The records themselves are mostly pretty banal and were it not for the occasional Louis solo it is unlikely that they would be of interest to even the most starry-eyed collector of old dance items. A recent discovery by the American collector Walter C. Allen is a very important one. It concerns a very rare master of Henderson's *Everybody Loves My Baby* (take one) on the Regal label, on which there are vocal breaks by Louis. It has been assumed for years that the first vocal which Louis recorded was *Gut Bucket Blues*, made on 12 November 1925, but the Henderson side pre-dates this by nine months. It had been known that *Everybody Loves My Baby* was one of the numbers that Henderson featured during stage shows, complete with a vocal chorus by Louis, but that it was actually recorded with vocal breaks is an unexpected disclosure.

In addition to the records he made with the Henderson band, Louis also went into the studios as an accompanist to some of the great blues singers of the day, usually with companions from the full orchestra. The titles he made with Bessie Smith are available to this day, but others with such vocalists as Clara Smith and Maggie Jones are undeservedly obscure. As a blues accompanist Louis was superb, filling in between phrases and providing entirely apt background statements that enhanced the work of the vocalist without conflicting with it. Sensitivity and warmth are the basic requirements for a blues accompaniment, and Louis was only rivalled in this role by Joe Smith and Tommy Ladnier, both of them also members at one time or another of Henderson's trumpet team. Readers will find recommended records for most of the periods discussed in this book in a separate listing at the close. In addition to these blues items Louis also recorded with Clarence Williams's Blue Five during 1924–25. The Williams group often included another great New Orleans musician, the late Sidney Bechet, and the music was very much akin to that of the New Orleans pioneers. In these congenial surroundings Louis must often have felt more at home than when he was playing with Henderson. One of the titles he

20

made with Williams was *Coal Cart Blues*, a reference to his early job driving a coal cart.

In 1925 Lil organized her own orchestra for an engagement at the Dreamland Café in Chicago and persuaded the owner to make Louis an offer of $75 a week if he would return from New York City and be featured with it. This was a very high salary at the time and at first Louis doubted the authenticity of the offer, but upon realizing that it was not a hoax he approached Henderson and obtained his release. The 14 November 1925 issue of the *Chicago Defender* carried an advertisement announcing that Lil's Dreamland Syncopators would include the 'World's Greatest Jazz Cornetist', Louis Armstrong. A week or two later the same paper carried a review of the band that asserted, of Louis, that 'This boy is in a class by himself.'

Within a few weeks of opening at the Dreamland, Erskine Tate booked Louis to appear with his Vendome Theatre Orchestra. For the first time Louis's extraordinary acting and singing ability was given full rein and it is said that many people came along to see the stage show and left before the film was shown. One of the routines Louis used here was the fairly common 'preaching' one during which he donned a frock-coat and delivered a mock sermon. A year or two later another famous trumpeter, the late 'Hot Lips' Page, stopped the show in Kansas City when, as a member of the Benny Moten band, he used the same routine. The Tate band had a large repertoire which

21

included light classic pieces, but the only two titles which Armstrong recorded with them are stomps.

On 12 November 1925 Armstrong recorded for the first time as a leader in his own right. He used a pick-up group of himself, the famous New Orleans trombonist Edward 'Kid' Ory, and three members of the Oliver band— Johnny Dodds, Johnny St. Cyr and Lil Hardin, his wife. The first number he recorded was *My Heart* and the name of his band was the 'Hot Five'. From this time until the December of 1927 he recorded fairly frequently with this line-up, sometimes enlarging the group by adding Pete Briggs on tuba and Warren 'Baby' Dodds on drums. During the same period he made numerous records as an accompanist to various blues singers, including Bertha 'Chippie' Hill, Hociel Thomas, Sippie Wallace and Nolan Welsh. It is unfortunate that the latter have not been reissued except on an occasional 'bootleg' label, for they include some of his most moving playing, but it is some compensation that almost all of the 'Hot Five' and 'Hot Seven' records are currently obtainable on microgroove.

So much has been written about these records that there is very little that one can add at this late date. Within a short while of any person becoming interested in jazz they gain an awareness of their importance and their ranking as jazz classics would hardly be challenged by any rational critic. Louis's companions were ideal for performances of the kind he desired, with Johnny Dodds outstanding. Ory was a good ensemble man, but his solos were restricted by

22

the tailgate style he used. Lil Hardin Armstrong was a good musician but as has been already indicated her roots were not in jazz to the same extent as the others. Finally, the New Orleans banjoist Johnny St. Cyr has not always received his share of praise for his role in the 'Hot Five' recordings. It is an arduous task to make a two-piece rhythm section sound full and to give a powerful three-piece front line a solid support, but it is a remarkable commentary on St. Cyr's musicianship that one is never at all conscious of any thinness in the rhythm support on these numbers. It is no slight to some excellent musicians when one says that Dodds was the only man who could keep up with Louis as a soloist on these records and that even he had his work cut out at times, for this was the period when Armstrong was not only developing personally into a remarkable virtuoso soloist but was also setting the style for all jazz trumpeters in a fashion which was to dominate the field for a decade or more. In a more roundabout fashion his playing at this time has formed a link with the art of jazz trumpet playing down to this very day.

The mention in the last paragraph of the ability of the musicians as *soloists* is made necessary by the fact that the tight ensemble qualities of the Oliver band were gradually being replaced by a much looser conception. Although Armstrong retained the traditional New Orleans front line of trumpet, trombone and clarinet, and some of the ensemble work is excellent, the very nature of his individual development was bound to result, in the long run, in the

23

breaking away from what was for him a restraining factor. Some purist critics have deplored this fact, and William Grossman and Jack Farrell, from the viewpoint of extreme New Orleans style partisanship, have devoted a chapter in their book *The Heart of Jazz* titled 'The Apostasy of Louis Armstrong' to a long jeremiad on Armstrong's refusal to keep within the 'pure' tradition. Leaving aside any disagreements with the position such purist critics maintain, it should be obvious to anyone familiar with Armstrong's work with Henderson, for example, that it must lead him towards the role of a virtuoso artist. The fact still remains that the 'Hot Five' and 'Hot Seven' records, despite more stress on solo playing, are amongst the greatest examples of New Orleans style jazz preserved.

The most casual listener cannot help but discern the increasing technical mastery and daringness of invention which Armstrong displays on these records. The first few sessions are probably tighter as far as the ensembles are concerned, although there are many glimpses of the dazzling solos that were to come. By 1927 Armstrong had become bolder and embroidered the themes with solos of astonishing power and invention. The later 'Hot Seven' period included such masterpieces as *Melancholy Blues*, *Wild Man Blues*, *Gully Low Blues* and *Potato Head Blues* and it is a tribute to their worth that they still sound fresh today. Johnny Dodds was a perfect foil for Armstrong on this type of number. He certainly lacked Armstrong's total

24

Louis Armstrong's Hot Five, *c.* 1926. Reading from left to right members are Johnny St. Cyr, Kid Ory, Louis Armstrong, Johnny Dodds, and Lil Hardin

Pace photo by Gilbert Gaster

Armstrong and Trummy Young at an informal session at the Humphrey Lyttelton club in Oxford Street, London, which some members of the Armstrong All Stars visited during their tour of England in 1956

instrumental command, but as a blues clarinettist he has never been equalled. His thick tone with its blues-based inflections was the antithesis of the lighter and more pure toned Creole tradition, and on the numbers like *High Society* which called for an approach which combined rapid fingering and a fluent style he was certainly not at his best; but he was one of the few men who could hold his own with Louis in an ensemble and I can think of nobody at that time who could have followed the trumpet solo on *Wild Man Blues* without creating an effect of utter anti-climax. The French critic André Hodeir has tended to ridicule what he considers to be Dodds's 'corny' work on these records, but M. Hodeir seems startlingly insensitive to early blues forms and cannot be counted a reliable judge of such records.

It should be made clear that these records were made with a group which played together only in a recording studio. It made one public appearance, on 12 June 1926, when it took part in a mammoth concert of 'race' artists who recorded for the Okeh company (Negro artists were usually assigned to a series which was identified with the title of 'race' by the record companies at this time). Many years later Kid Ory recalled how easy these sessions were to make and it is still impossible to decide how much is owed to the Negro pianist Richard M. Jones who was in charge of this department of Okeh records at the time. There can be no doubt that his giving the artists freedom to record what they wished without any irritating restrictions

25

must have helped immeasurably in the quality of the music that resulted.

It was only natural that Armstrong's great reputation should tempt other trumpeters to try to defeat him in a battle of music, or 'cutting contest' as it was called. Kid Ory, in a discussion with Dick Hadlock in the *Down Beat* of 8 January 1959, refers to an attempt by another virtuoso trumpeter of the period, Jabbo Smith, to get the better of Armstrong. 'One time in Chicago', he recalled, 'Jabbo Smith came in with blood in his eyes for Louis, thinking he would blow him out. When Louis finished playing, Jabbo said, "I'm gonna get a trombone." Johnny Dunn tried to take Louis, too. Same thing.' An amusing story relates to the latter attempt. At this time Johnny Dunn was the great man in the north and it is said that when he arrived at a Chicago station, bearing a yard-long coach horn which he used during his stage shows, he ran into the flamboyant Jelly Roll Morton. Morton eyed the coach horn and advised Dunn 'to take that thing right back to New York. These Chicago boys will cut you to death!'

A final note on the 'Hot Seven' records is left to the modernist trumpeter Miles Davis in *Jazz Review*, dated December 1958. The U.S. critic Nat Hentoff played Davis the 1927 Armstrong version of *Potato Head Blues*. Davis commented as follows:

'Louis has been through all kinds of styles. That's good tuba by the way. You know you can't play anything on a horn that Louis hasn't played—I mean even modern. I love his approach to the trumpet; he never sounds bad. He plays on the beat and you can't miss when you play on the beat—with feeling. That's another phrase for swing.

'There's form there, and you take some of those early forms, play it today, and they'd sound good. I also like the little stops in his solo. We stop, but we often let the drums lay out altogether. If I had this record, I'd play it.'

To return to Louis's career during this period. During the spring of 1926 Armstrong left the Dreamland and joined Carroll Dickerson's orchestra at the Sunset Café, still retaining his other job with the Erskine Tate Vendome orchestra. By chance, just across the street was the Plantation Café and the band there was led by King Oliver. It was in Dickerson's band that Armstrong met the great pianist Earl Hines who was soon to be associated with him and to appear on many of his most famous records. He first recorded with Hines on 9 May 1927 when he made a single side, *Chicago Breakdown*, with a group other than his usual regular recording band. Early in 1927 Dickerson left the job and Armstrong took over the band and reorganized it. The manager and owner of the Sunset Café was Joe Glaser, now a famous booker and Armstrong's current manager. Sometime in 1927 Louis finally left the Vendome band, but became a regular attraction during the afternoon and evenings at the Metropolitan Theatre. When his band closed at the Sunset there came a little known interlude, told by William Russell in *Jazzmen*, when he hired the Warwick Hall and led his own group there. The venture was not successful and soon folded. In April 1928 Louis rejoined Carroll Dickerson's band at Chicago's Savoy Ballroom and gained more public acclaim than ever. Russell records that he left the Savoy for two nights to work a job in St. Louis which paid him a hundred dollars a night plus expenses—unheard of remuneration for that time. He received another offer from Fletcher Henderson at this time and the Savoy were forced to give him a considerable increase to prevent his acceptance. In addition to the regular patrons, musicians were flocking to hear Louis, and by word of mouth his fame spread across the country. It was, therefore, only natural that he should sooner or later go to New York City, and this move took place in 1929. But before writing of this it might be as well to mention some of the numbers that Louis recorded during 1928.

The last of the 'Hot Five' sessions took place in December 1927. On 26 June 1928 Louis was part of an instrumental quartet which accompanied the singer Lillie Delk Christian on four somewhat undistinguished titles. It is interesting to note that one of the musicians on this date was the great New Orleans clarinettist Jimmy Noone. The next day came the first of a series of recordings issued under the title of 'Louis Armstrong and his Hot Five' or 'Louis Armstrong and his Savoy Ballroom Five' which, despite the initial group name, were entirely different in character from anything he had done before. The front line

instrumentation of trumpet, trombone and clarinet (
doubling on tenor saxophone) was retained but I
Robinson and Jimmy Strong, who played trombone and
clarinet respectively, were good competent musicians in
a style that owed little to that of their predecessors Ory
and Dodds. Mancy Cara was on banjo, but the real stars
of the band apart from Armstrong himself, were Earl
Hines and drummer Zutty Singleton. The latter had come
up from New Orleans a year before and was a remarkably
consistent drummer whose style suited the group Louis led
at the time as almost no other drummer's could. He was
much in advance in certain ways of most of the earlier
drummers and until a disagreement some years later
was Armstrong's constant companion for a lengthy period.
If Zutty provided the firm foundation for the group,
in Earl Hines Louis had found a musician who could
match his own dazzling solos. Much has been made of
Hines's supposed debt to Armstrong and the development
of what has been called his 'trumpet style' of piano playing,
but it is more likely true that Hines would have played the
way he does even if he had never appeared with Armstrong
at all in the twenties. Hines is himself a virtuoso performer
whose nonchalance of approach can often lead one to miss
the sheer technical command of his solos. He is a master
at suspending the beat during a solo for a number of bars,
causing the listener to suspect that he has lost it altogether,
but invariably he returns to it with an unerring instinct at
the appropriate bar. This device is one which creates

tension in the best sense of the word, but it is a tension which is always resolved. His unflagging invention and his hard hit treble passages create great excitement for the listener and when I last heard him, in San Francisco during October 1958, although he was playing with an extremely indifferent band his own work was as scintillating as ever.

With companions of varying stature it was only natural that the records which Armstrong made should place even greater emphasis on the solo routines. As already indicated, Robinson and Strong were highly competent performers, but by comparison with Armstrong and Hines they were minor figures. One of the first titles that the six-piece group made is one of Armstrong's most famous, *West End Blues*. This is a slow, rather melancholy theme which includes a moving scat vocal by Louis and a solo that is justly renowned. The other numbers tended to be faster in tempo and gave scope for Hines and Armstrong to create solos of brilliance. A further departure from the New Orleans tradition was taken when Don Redman was added to the band as arranger and alto saxophonist. This was the first time that Armstrong had used an arranger but Redman's scores were simple and allowed plenty of scope for improvised solos. An example of Armstrong's increasing technical mastery and daring is *Tight Like This*, the last number he was to record with Hines for some years, where he builds up a solo of several choruses at the close which have an almost architectural solidity of structure. The logic of

30

this particular solo is as remarkable as almost anyt[...]
he has recorded. Although the overall impact of the
records may not be quite as great as that of the earlier ones
with Dodds and Ory, they show that Armstrong had now
left the traditional New Orleans concept far behind.

The Savoy engagement was terminated in the spring of
1929 and the members of the band decided to remain together and, nominating Armstrong as the official leader,
thought that the time had come to try their luck in New
York. Their departure was somewhat eccentric. Louis
owned a broken-down car which he used to drive himself,
Hines and Singleton around in, and other members of the
band possessed cars of equally dubious reliability. Lil
managed to assemble a total of twenty dollars for each
man, and they started the journey to New York. They did
finally arrive there, most of them penniless, but there were
various problems to face before they were out of trouble.
Their first engagement was at the Aubudon Theatre in the
Bronx, but when the time came for them to play the date
there was great trouble in rounding up the various members
of the band who had dispersed in search of other work.
Jimmy Harrison had to be brought in on trombone, but
when they finally played *St. Louis Blues* as their number
at the theatre there was no doubt about their success.
A week later they obtained a job at the famous Savoy
Ballroom in Harlem and continuing success here led to
a very good job at Connie's Inn. A short while afterwards
Armstrong himself was booked to appear in the Broadway

31

revue 'Hot Chocolates'. This resulted in his acceptance by a section of the general public who might never have heard of him otherwise, and it was a key event in his career. He sang and played *Ain't Misbehavin'* in the show and his record of this became one of his first popular sellers. From this time onwards Louis became a stage and show personality in his own right and in the years that followed he was gradually to break into all the fields that an entertainer finds open to him. Even so, he was still a long way from the international eminence that he enjoys today.

Soon after his arrival in New York he recorded with one of the first mixed groups to gather in a studio. The title that was issued from this session, *Knockin' a Jug*, is still highly regarded at the present time, and marked the first collaboration between Louis and the great white trombonist Jack Teagarden. He also recorded quite prolifically with a larger band and often used the Luis Russell group. The second 'Hot Five' made its last records on 10 June 1929, accompanying the blues singer Victoria Spivey on two numbers. Gene Anderson replaced Earl Hines, who had not left Chicago with the rest of the band. It was to be many years before Louis was again to record with a regular small group, and the next two decades were to see him fronting a number of large bands. On the records he was now making the band played a very subsidiary role in the main, the accent being strongly on Armstrong as a solo performer. His material was changing also, comprising a high proportion of popular hit songs of the day. It should be noted that the popular songs of the late 'twenties seem, in retrospect, to be considerably less inane than those of the present time and many had a structure that was ideal for the improvising jazzman. On *Song of the Islands* Louis even added three violins to his recording band (Luis Russell's orchestra in this instance) and a few weeks later made his famous trumpet–piano duet with Buck Washington of *Dear Old Southland*. It says much for his popularity that he recorded steadily during the depression years when the sales of gramophone records touched rock bottom.

The engagement at Connie's Inn terminated in the early summer of 1930 and Louis left New York for California. He was now determined to exploit his success to date and the next few years were to see him travelling extensively. It was only eight years since he had come to Chicago to join King Oliver, but he had revolutionized the concept of jazz trumpet playing during that period.

3

1930-35 — THE VIRTUOSO PERIOD

Louis Armstrong arrived in Los Angeles in June 1930 and started a long engagement at the 'Sebastian New Cotton Club'. At this time he was booked as a single and fronted the house band. Some confusion exists as to the actual leader of the band when he first arrived, Louis himself claiming that the director was 'some old trumpet player named Elkins'. Whoever the mysterious Elkins might have been there is no evidence that he was in any group with whom Louis recorded at this time. Recent investigation has proved that the two bands with whom Louis recorded in Los Angeles were led by Leon Heriford and Les Hite, and both were the house bands at the 'New Cotton Club' during part of Louis's stay. Throughout the years Louis has often left the selection of the musicians to others and has been content to front a band that was already in existence. Orin Keepnews, in the *Record Changer* of July–August 1950, has quoted him on the subject, as follows:

'I picked my own men to an extent, but I never did

34

want to bother about all that other unnecessary business. So I always had a leader or a director—someone like Randolph, or Joe Garland, or Mike McKendrick—so when anybody was dissatisfied, they'd come to him to straighten it all out.'

The records Louis made in California are mostly of popular songs like *Body and Soul* and *Memories of You*. They contain excellent solos but are not great records overall. From about 1928 Louis had become enamoured of the sound of Guy Lombardo's saxophone section and in the issue of the *Record Changer* already mentioned he was tackled about the matter. For the benefit of readers unaware of Guy Lombardo it should be mentioned that he has been famous throughout the years as the purveyor of a brand of dance music noted for its extreme sentimentality and 'sweet' approach. Louis had the following to say about the Lombardo influence on his bands:

'Now you dig that *Sweethearts*, and that first chorus of *When You're Smiling*; it reminds you of Guy Lombardo. Crawford Wethington, who played with my band then, he was the nearest thing to Carmen Lombardo.

'When we were at the Savoy in Chicago, in 1928, every Sunday night we'd catch the Owl Club, with Guy Lombardo, and as long as he played we'd sit right there: Zutty, Carroll Dickerson and all the band. We didn't go nowhere until after Lombardo signed off. That went on for months. Music for me, music that's good, you just want to hear it again!'

Jazz musicians show an obstinate refusal to conform to any purist notions that their fans may hold. Charlie Parker was a great admirer of Jimmy Dorsey, Lester Young liked a lot of somewhat dubious popular vocalists, and the list of apparently incompatible tastes could be lengthened to include many of the great jazz stars. Most jazz musicians see themselves as part of the larger field of entertainment and it is a comparatively recent development for many of them to take themselves seriously as 'artists'. If their own evaluation of themselves were more widely accepted many a disillusioned fan would be saved much anguish!

While in Los Angeles Louis recorded for the first time with Lionel Hampton—the solo in *Memories of You* was the first that the latter had recorded on vibraphone—and with Lawrence Brown who was later to become famous as a member of the Duke Ellington orchestra. At the end of the job at the 'Cotton Club' Louis went back to Chicago and formed a band there, the actual musical director being the trumpeter Zilner Randolph. On the whole this was a rather mediocre group, but some good records were made by it. Louis played around Chicago most of the time, but made one triumphant return to New Orleans, appearing at the Suburban Gardens. During 1930 and 1931 he also took part in a few short feature films and it would be interesting to have these shown again if there are copies still in existence.

In 1932 Louis made his first foreign tour, coming to

England and playing at the London Palladium with a local group. The reactions were varied and it is apparent from reading the musical press of that time that even the critics were bewildered by much that they heard. Stories have grown up around this visit that are probably apocryphal, one such dealing with the time that he was challenged by another musician on the ground that he was attaining his high notes by the use of a freak instrument. The story has it that he smashed his instrument to pieces on the spot and went on with the show on a borrowed trumpet. The *Melody Maker* of the time does document his appearance, as a guest, at a brass band rally! It is stated that the stolid brass bandsmen were unimpressed by what they heard of him.

Returning to America Louis took over the Chick Webb band and made one recording session with them. Early in 1933 he went back to Chicago and formed another band made up of local musicians. I talked to Teddy Wilson about this period during a visit to the U.S.A. and he told me that at the time Louis was studying quite hard and was generally of a quiet and studious disposition. Wilson thought that the showmanship that is so much a part of Louis's current act came much later, although this is contradicted by the testimony of other musicians. The truth is that there was always a large element of hokum in the New Orleans days—the great King Oliver was apparently not averse to placing a mute in his cornet and giving out imitations of a donkey braying—and it is natural for musicians from this era to exploit any talents that they may possess in this direction. The records which Louis made at this time for the Victor label are generally rated as amongst his least successful by collectors, and many people dislike the exhibitionism that is so much a part of them.

It seems certain that the batch of records made between January and April 1933 reflect Louis's performances of the period quite faithfully. We have the testimony of Milton 'Mezz' Mezzrow, in his book *Really the Blues*, that Louis often arrived at the studio without knowing what he was going to play and that the amount of time devoted to rehearsal was minimal in the extreme. The numbers performed included several very undistinguished, to put it no more strongly, pops. Yet, seen against Armstrong's career as a whole this was a phase through which it was more or less inevitable that he should pass. For several years he had been developing as an instrumentalist and he now had a command that would have been unthinkable to the earlier New Orleans men. It seems a corollary of technical advance that there will be a misuse of some element of it, and it also seems to be the case that even the greatest musicians are inclined to show lapses of taste, sometimes the greater the musician the more glaring their lapses are. By 1933 Armstrong had discovered that he could play in the upper register of his instrument with consummate ease. He also found that long high note codas went down well with the crowds that came to his stage shows. It became known that he featured these high note endings and what was more natural than that he should incorporate them into his records? At the same time there is a tendency to regard the use of high notes as being in poor taste under *any* circumstances. This is a ridiculous outlook, for occasionally they can be effective at the end of a logically developed solo or even as a means of increasing tension midway through a chorus. Even when used as a showy effect they can be quite a valid means to an end during a stage performance. It is only when they become an end in themselves, as on Charlie Barnet's *All the Things You Are* for example, that their use is entirely pointless. A good instance of the valid use of extreme high register notes can be heard in the closing bars of *Madness in Great Ones* from Duke Ellington's *Such Sweet Thunder* suite. It is unfortunate that the whole question has become confused by the puritanism that seems to accompany so much jazz criticism these days.

On the Victor records Louis sometimes used high notes to no good purpose, as in the coda of *Sittin' in the Dark*. On the other hand, on a number like *I Gotta Right to Sing the Blues* he uses them quite logically and to telling effect. In fact, this latter performance is a remarkable one in every way. The solo that Louis builds here is one of the most powerful he has ever recorded and the rather poor band is forgotten when he begins to build his choruses. There are other numbers on which he plays very well indeed, but it would be true to say that the band is as

39

ragged as any he has fronted and had few other soloists of any merit. The records as a whole are certainly not amongst Louis's great ones—although the strength of his solo on *I Gotta Right to Sing the Blues* is such that I rate this amongst his finest individual performances—but they are not as bad as many critics would have one believe. The fact is that Armstrong is such an extraordinary artist that very few of his considerable number of records are utterly without interest.

The thirties saw Louis influencing a whole new group of trumpeters and, indeed, musicians on all instruments. Although some critics have tended to write of nearly all this period as a time when he was more concerned with showy effects than playing what they like to consider real jazz, musicians saw it quite differently. Roy Eldridge, in the course of a conversation with the critic Nat Hentoff, reminisced about his early days and the time when he was buying the 'Hot Seven' records. He went on to say:

'But Louis wasn't an influence on me until I saw him in person. Jabbo Smith didn't have Louis's sound, but he was faster. But Louis gave me something I couldn't get off Jabbo—continuity, which makes all the sense. Louis introduces the piece and sticks around the melody, but when he has it out, you know it's out, and you know he's going to finish a whole.

'In 1932, I first caught Louis at the Lafayette Theatre in New York, and he finally upset me. I was a young cat, and I was very fast, but I wasn't telling no kind of story.

40

Columbia Records photo by Don Hunstein

Louis Armstrong in 1959

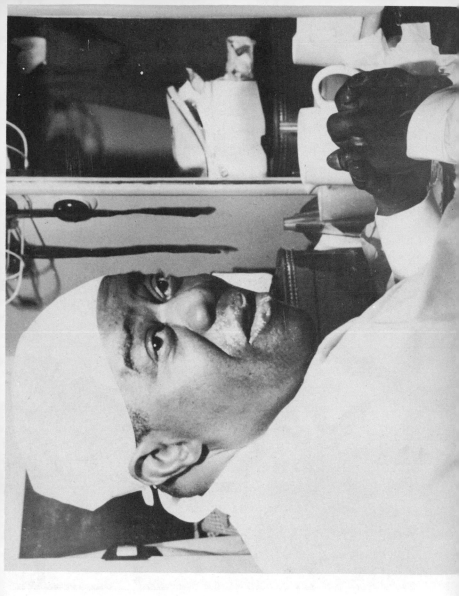

Louis Armstrong's dressing-room preparations prior to a public performance assume a ritualistic character. This photo was taken by Ken Palmer during Armstrong's British tour in 1959

Well, I sat through the first show, and I didn't think Louis was so extraordinary. But in the second show, he played *Chinatown*. He started out like a new book, building and building, chorus after chorus, and finally reaching a full climax, ending on his high F. It was a real climax, right, clean, clear. The rhythm was rocking, and he had that sound going along with it. Everybody was standing up, including me. He was building the thing all the time instead of just playing in a straight line.'

Eldridge has touched here on an essential point of the high note controversy, for as often as not at this period Louis built to his upper register endings absolutely logically and, what is more, made them cleanly and clearly. One of the astonishing aspects of his playing is that his tone is as fine in the upper register as it is when he is playing in the medium range. In later years Louis was to feature high notes less and less, his style having become more simplified and the advance of age resulting in greater maturity. His influence on trumpet playing as a whole was mentioned by the ex-Ellington star Rex Stewart in *Down Beat* of 8 January 1950. He had the following to say:

'Seriously, I really feel that without his influence, I couldn't imagine what trumpet playing would be like. He showed that there was more range than high C, and more drive than the syncopation used before him. He did so many things. . . .'

The reason for bringing in a discussion of high note technique and the question of showmanship at this stage

41

is that, despite the fact that many of the records that Louis made during the 'thirties are not counted amongst his finest work, it was probably at this time that he had the maximum influence on other musicians. It was quite common for the bigger bands of that period to carry a trumpeter whose playing was modelled on Louis and, as often as not, one who would sing in the Armstrong style. Taft Jordan started out with Chick Webb as a pure Louis imitator and in this country there were people like Nat Gonella who modelled themselves on him. As is often the case, it is the technical side of a man's playing that has the greatest influence on others, but something of the spirit with which he approached a number was captured by some of the men who admired him. A trumpeter like Ruby Braff is playing today in a style very much influenced by Armstrong, but aside from the technical debt he owes to him he also captures a little of the spirit that makes an Armstrong solo such a rewarding experience. Generally, though, apart from the revivalist musicians who have moved on to what is now called a 'mainstream' style, Armstrong's *direct* influence on other trumpeters is now slight. The reason is, of course, the almost complete enslavement of young modernist players to the concepts that arose out of the bop revolution. This will be briefly mentioned in the final section of the book.

Resuming the outline of Armstrong's career, it appears that the first trip to England had convinced him that the time was propitious for a longer tour, and in July 1933 he commenced his second European visit with a London appearance. This time he was again greeted with mixed reviews, for the more serious jazz followers who must have comprised a sizeable segment of his audiences found themselves unable to accept the high proportion of showmanship in his act and there were laments over his failure to size up the audiences to whom he would be playing. In his *Jazz in Britain* David Boulton suggests that one of the reasons might have been that British audiences had just had the opportunity of hearing the Duke Ellington band and were under the sway of Ellington's less flamboyant presentation, but Mr. Boulton forgets that Ellington himself had been criticized for the unadventurousness of *his* programmes and his tendency to play for safety by sticking to familiar material. History certainly does repeat itself in this connexion and virtually every tour undertaken by an American group in the past few years has been adversely reported on by some members of the jazz public for just such a failing. The *Melody Maker* of 5 August 1933 carried the following somewhat disillusioned report on an Armstrong concert:

'He seems to have come to the conclusion that a variety artist's only mission in life is to be sensational, to pander to the baser emotions, to sacrifice all art to crude showmanship.'

Apart from the matter of correctly gauging his audience, Armstrong had other troubles at this time. He was involved in a dispute with his manager, Jack Collins, and the partnership of some years was abruptly terminated, with Jack Hylton taking over his business management. After he had been here nearly a year, fronting various pick-up groups all the while, Coleman Hawkins arrived in London. Hawkins, who had revolutionized the playing of the tenor saxophone in jazz as Armstrong had, in his turn, the trumpet, was scheduled to join Louis for the final part of his tour and arrangements were announced for the first of their joint appearances. Just a few days before it should have taken place Armstrong refused to go ahead and considerable ill-will was engendered as a result. It has never been explained why Armstrong acted as he did, but considering that it is quite contrary to all that is known of him to refuse to fulfil commitments to which he has already given assent, one must presume that he was reacting to pressures which he did not care to publicize. All this had little effect on his actual playing and he reverted to a less sensational presentation after the initial criticisms had been voiced. A very interesting comment by Harry Dial, drummer with the band that Louis was leading just prior to his coming to England, proves that Louis was well aware of the musical deficiencies of his normal stage routine, and are worth quoting in full. They were contained in an interview which the American collector Frank Driggs had with Dial which was reproduced in *Jazz Journal* of January 1959, as follows:

'When I got there the band was really putrid. I thought for a couple of years that the band was slipping because

44

Louis had gone in for all the showmanship stuff, you know, high notes, gestures, and I thought he couldn't play any more. I soon lost that opinion when I began working with him. We used to get out in those little towns in the mid-west where people didn't know him too well and didn't pay much attention to the show, so he'd sit down and really play horn. He had special numbers for musicians who would drop by and listen to him. He'd play *High Society* and *Tiger Rag*, which used to work the stew out of any drummer, because he'd never stop where he'd say he was going to. He'd have a certain place where he'd want you to ride the cymbal. He'd hit as many as 350 high Cs on *Shine*, I used to count them. He'd make me so mad on *Tiger Rag* that I wouldn't know what to do. He'd want me to ride the cymbals on the last three choruses, and you'd swear he wasn't going to play more than ten choruses on *Tiger Rag*. I'd grab the cymbal around the 8th chorus and start riding it . . . 8 . . . 9 . . . 10 and by the end of the tenth chorus it would sound good to him. The end of the 11th, and he'd play ten more choruses!'

It is something of a mystery what the variety theatre patrons in this country really thought of Louis but to all intents and purposes he had a successful tour. He went over to the Continent after the English circuits had been exhausted and played two memorable concerts at the Salle Pleyel, Paris, in November 1934. While in Paris he recorded for the first time in eighteen months—one of the longest gaps in his recording career—and of the six titles made, *On the Sunny Side of the Street* has become something of a classic. Perhaps no other single recording gives so accurate a portrayal of the performances which Armstrong was featuring at this time. Two other titles from the session—*Song of the Vipers* and *Will You, Won't You Be My Baby*—were deleted within a day or two of the original issue and until they were reissued in the late 'forties remained amongst his rarest items. Upon hearing them now it is not apparent as to why they were withdrawn, unless exception was taken to the reference to vipers (marihuana smokers).

Armstrong was away from the United States for just over eighteen months, his longest absence ever, but homesickness at last caused him to return, and in January 1935 he arrived back in New York City. At that time nobody knew it, but this was to be the end of the pure virtuoso phase, and in the next year Armstrong's style was to undergo a change in the direction of greater simplicity, while his tone was to become less cloudy than it had been in the past five years. Whenever an artist varies a style there will be found those who regard it as proof of musical deterioration, and as we shall see, his new approach was poorly understood at first.

4

1935-47 —
JAZZ STAR AND ENTERTAINER

For the first few months of 1935 Armstrong was forced to rest as the result of a split lip. Strange rumours circulated in Europe about the nature of his illness and one newspaper reported his death! However, it was a comparatively short while before Louis was again ready to take to the road with a big band, and it was Luis Russell's orchestra that he fronted when he was once more completely fit. This association with Russell was to continue for over a decade and many famous musicians were to be members of the band during this period. A recording contract with the Decca company followed, and with only occasional breaks, has been renewed down to the present time.

To describe the period of the late 'thirties as an interim one for Armstrong does not imply that he was no longer playing well or making worthwhile records, but is meant to refer to the fact that his later eminence had not yet been attained, while the more purist jazz followers were somewhat dismayed by the 'commercial' records that he so often turned out. What so many of the objectors had not yet realized was that many of their most highly prized records were of popular tunes of the day, but that they themselves were far enough away from the period not to recognize them as such. The length of time it takes for a popular song to become a 'standard' has never been accurately measured, but one wonders how many people have denounced a number on its first appearance as just another hit song, only to enjoy it years afterwards and, quite probably, claim that it was proof of the superiority of the popular song in the past over that of the present!

In the decade now under review a very high proportion of Armstrong's records, and the stage and show presentations he took part in, featured popular song material and it might be as well to consider some of the viewpoints of the jazz follower in relationship to the popular number. My personal attitude is that Armstrong has such an ability to transform the *content* of a popular hit, both in his trumpet and vocal interpretation, that I am not usually disturbed by such considerations as an inane lyric or a song content that may be basically undesirable. This is not to say that I am never perturbed at Armstrong's material. In the period of which I write the popular song, although often banal, had not reached the depths of trashiness of the present day and many made quite suitable vehicles for a jazz performer. Louis's unique vocal talents take the sentimentality out of nearly all the popular songs he has

used on record and it is only occasionally that he has selected, or had selected for him, a number so poor that even he could do nothing with it. That there are some jazz standards and popular songs, graced with the title of a standard through use over the years, that appear ideally suited to Armstrong I would not deny, but even this supposition is sometimes open to doubt in relationship to the real worth of the numbers. I think that one tends to overemphasize the merit of certain songs just because Armstrong has used them as the basis of an exceptional performance. Even the finest popular song shows up badly as against the best numbers of a Duke Ellington, for instance, but over the years the truly outstanding jazz musician has always had the ability to make routine material sound better than it really is. A performer of Armstrong's type can play a melody *almost* straight but it is the fractional differences of inflexion that result in a performance that is outside the normal run of dance band routines. The whole problem cannot be seen clearly unless one takes into account the nature of the performer, for while one would be dismayed to hear a unique orchestra like Duke Ellington's confined to the popular song, great musicians like Armstrong, Hawkins and Earl Hines have been quite happy to use them and have, in the process of their solos, stripped them of over-sentimentality or banality. Collectors are apt to forget that even if one ignores the high proportion of popular material that Armstrong used from about 1929, the fact remains that quite a few of the

49

earlier 'classic Hot Five' records use such material. It is, as I have already remarked, all a question of how far one is from the period when a song is current. It is also not inappropriate to mention that this is a period when 'original' compositions appear on nearly every new long playing record by jazz musicians, and the dullness of these themes is well enough known. Jazz has had very few exceptional composers and most jazz musicians write themes inferior to those of the better popular songwriters. The key to the problem lies in the treatment afforded to the songs, and it is certainly true that at the present time many vocalists are hailed as jazz performers when, in truth, they are above-average pop singers. However, I do not think that Armstrong can be accused of excessive respect for popular material, and the use he has made of it has nearly always been of a jazz nature. The reason why collectors were unhappy when Armstrong's Decca recordings were first available is that the songs used were contemporaneous, not because they were popular songs as such.

It is somewhat interesting to note that one of the titles that Armstrong recorded at his first Decca session, in October 1935, was *On Treasure Island*, which he himself once said was one of his favourite records. The short but succinct reaction of one reviewer to the first Decca items to be issued in this country can be quoted from the January–February 1936 issue of *Swing Music*:

'The first titles are unbelievably bad. *Brand New Suit* has a grand swing opening, and Louis is Louis, but not at

his best. The record just fades away towards the end.'

A few months later a reviewer in the same magazine, Eric Ballard, was expressing a different viewpoint and it is to his credit that he was one of the first critics apart from Hugues Panassié to realize that the changes that had taken place in Armstrong's playing were not necessarily for the worse. In the course of a review he had the following to say:

'This is not the old Armstrong. Louis is not playing the trumpet of his so-called "better" days, as I have heard it contended. He is playing trumpet in a way that we have never heard before. His tone is different; his ideas are new; only his method is the same.

'Harlem has been waiting a long time to hear Louis, and Harlem was reserving judgment until it had heard him. Ready to put him back on top if it thought fit, but just as ready to write him off as a back number if he failed to please. And what was Harlem's reception? You all know. Louis Armstrong is today more certainly the king of modern music than he ever was before. He is still so far ahead of the next best that any kind of comparison is impossible.'

This summary is actually a little extreme as far as the records are concerned, for while it is true that there are some very good solos by Armstrong on the records in question it was to be a year or two before the full flowering of the new style was to be heard. Of one fact there can be little doubt, and that is that the Luis Russell band at this

51

period was at the lowest peak in its history. It had a sound rhythm section and one good soloist in Charlie Holmes, but the ensemble quality was deplorable, and rather understandably, such numbers as *Red Sails in the Sunset*, *Old Man Mose* and *La Cucaracha* were hardly of the type to inspire any arranger. In addition the actual recording quality of many of the discs was poor, for it is a curious fact that many records made in 1927 and 1928 are much superior in this respect to those made a decade later when it might have been expected that advances in techniques would have ensured a higher quality of sound. If one looks down the list of titles Armstrong made during 1935 and 1936 there are few which one would unhesitatingly recommend for reissue today judged as overall performances.

Swing that Music, recorded in April 1936, was made to coincide with the appearance of a book bearing the same title and having Armstrong's name as the author. As already indicated in the introduction it seems somewhat unlikely that Armstrong in fact had much to do with the book. The style of writing is not his—and that style is as unique as his trumpet playing—while the impression the volume gives is of a not very competent hack job undertaken by a ghost writer. What is of interest is that by now Armstrong was a sufficiently established name to warrant a book being published under his nominal authorship. It was around the same time that Armstrong was first prominently credited in a film—he had previously made some now forgotten 'shorts' in the early 'thirties—the occasion

52

being the Bing Crosby–Frances Langford feature *Pennies From Heaven*. Armstrong's role in this film was not a very lengthy one and it was typical of a Hollywood attitude to jazz musicians that has prevailed down to the present day that it should be a comic one hardly designed to show the Negro as other than a buffoon, but it set Louis upon a film career that must be personally lucrative if artistically somewhat barren. In the film he appeared as a vocalist and trumpeter during a number called *Skeleton In The Closet* (altered by the more prudish British record company to *Skeleton In The Cupboard* when it first appeared in this country!) and in a couple of other scenes. In the following two years he had short scenes in four other films, *Artists and Models*, *Every Day's A Holiday* (1937), *Doctor Rhythm*, *Goin' Places* (1938). In none of them was any real advantage taken of his unique abilities as a jazz musician or even of his natural flair for showmanship, but they did have the result of his becoming known to audiences throughout the world who were hardly interested in jazz as such. It is possible that Armstrong's roles in these films, and later ones, were to provide some of the basis for criticisms of his stage personality as representing 'Uncle Tomism' in the years to follow, although at this time the criticisms made were directed at the film companies and not at Armstrong himself.

The period from 1937 onwards saw Armstrong making records that were aimed at a wide public, with a miscellany of backings. Although he had recorded many popular titles in the past, as already discussed, it is unlikely that they sold much to the public who wanted a version of the latest hit, but from now on he became as much a popular entertainer as jazz musician. There is not the contradiction involved in the two roles that many jazz fans would have one believe, for it was to be a few years yet before there arose a whole group of musicians who thought of themselves primarily as artists. Whatever the position was amongst themselves as far as merit was concerned, jazz players from the earliest New Orleans days had accepted that their public role was essentially that of an entertainer. If they struck an indifferent audience they probably played less well than they would to an enthusiastic one, but it did not occur to them to berate the unresponsive ones as lacking awareness of their music. Also, it would be extraordinary if Armstrong was totally unaware of the financial rewards to be obtained from widening his audience, with its possibilities in the way of radio and film work. His first records made with an unusual backing were the four titles with Hawaiian bands recorded in August 1936. In April 1937 he made four numbers with the popular Mills Brothers vocal quartet, recording with them again in 1938 and 1940. In June 1938 he made four spiritual numbers with the Decca Mixed Chorus and these sides are popular to this day, appearing on such apparently unlikely programmes as the BBC's 'Housewives' Choice'. Two months later he made two humorous monologues with Harry Mills, much to the horror of his purist followers. However, it is apt to

54

be forgotten that he still turned out consistently good jazz records during this time and only recently have a new generation of jazz record buyers begun to realize the quality of many of the Decca sides.

In 1937 there were changes in the Russell band and musicians of the calibre of J. C. Higginbotham, Albert Nicholas and Henry Allen were brought in to help raise the somewhat deplorable standard of the group. Armstrong himself seems to have been inspired by these changes, for his playing became much stronger and some of his solos, although more sober in style, have the majesty and power of his earlier classic performances. A really remarkable solo by him can be heard on his Decca version of *Struttin' With Some Barbecue*, where be builds chorus upon chorus at the close of the record in a most dazzling fashion. In the late 'thirties he began to re-record numbers which had been associated with him in the past, of the calibre of *Confessin'*, *West End Blues* and *Our Monday Date*. They formed a minority of his recordings at the time but a policy was inaugurated which in another decade was to be the cause of a great deal of argument amongst jazz fans in his concert audiences. It was at this time that I first heard the criticism that he was not improvising as much as he should and this is a matter which will be discussed in some detail in the next chapter.

In view of the lengthy period of fronting large bands it is interesting to note what Armstrong said on the subject in 1950 when asked if he preferred playing with a large or small group. The answer was printed in the *Record Changer* of July–August 1950:

'It don't really make no difference where I blow my horn as long as the guys behind me are playing right. But still and all I prefer the small band. I've had some good big bands; they were well rehearsed. But a leader's got to be able to instil himself into the band. Where there's too many men it's hard to get that *feeling*, like Joe Oliver and I had, like Jack (Teagarden) and I have.'

When I was in the U.S.A. in 1958 one musician who played in the big band Louis was fronting around 1939 intimated that he did not think that Louis was doing too well financially at the end of the 'thirties, but it is somewhat difficult to reconcile this with his film and radio appearances and the fact that the band worked steadily all the year round. This was still an era when the big band was supreme and there were theatres and dance halls throughout the U.S.A. booking them regularly. It is probable that the musician has confused the fact that Louis did not then have his vast public following of today, although his wide popularity by this time can hardly be denied. These years were comparatively tranquil ones for Armstrong compared with what was to happen in the next two decades, but he was fully employed moving from one city to another and taking the time out for the growing frequency of his film appearances.

In May 1940 Armstrong recorded with a small group again for an album of 'New Orleans Jazz' that Decca were planning. His companions included the great New Orleans veteran Sidney Bechet, and his drummer from the 'Savoy Ballroom Five' days, Zutty Singleton. One title he made was *Coal Cart Blues*, first recorded by him with Clarence Williams's Blue Five in 1924, and this is generally said to have been inspired by his youthful days when one of his jobs was delivering coal. In March and April of 1941 he recorded again with a group calling itself 'Louis Armstrong and his Hot Seven', but although one or two titles were good, the music was far below that of the original band of the same name. In 1942 a dispute between the American Federation of Musicians and the recording companies resulted in the former forbidding its members to make further records and, as a result, Armstrong was out of the studios for nearly three years. However, although he was not recording commercially, this was a period of intense activity for Armstrong.

Before dealing with the war years reference should be made to his one appearance as a stage actor, playing the role of Bottom in the play *Swingin' the Dream* at the Centre Theatre, New York City in 1939. The play had a very short run and although some of the theatre critics praised Armstrong it appears that the production as a whole was rather mediocre.

Following the bombing of Pearl Harbour the United States entered the war. The impact on the entertainment industry was drastic and the big bands were hit more badly than others. Key musicians were called up, touring became difficult and hazardous, while the quality of the music suffered as a result. Armstrong himself seems to have surmounted the difficulties very well and continued touring with a big band throughout the war years. The jazz world, however, was itself torn by the advent of a style of jazz initially called bop. This resulted from the searching experiments of musicians like Thelonious Monk, Clyde Hart, Dizzy Gillespie and Charlie Parker, and after at first meeting public hostility it was taken up enthusiastically by many critics and magazines of the time. In a decade and a half the work of the pioneers in the idiom was to lead to 'modern' jazz becoming the norm for most critics and jazz followers in the U.S.A. At the time of its appearance it split the jazz fans into two warring factions, one of which heralded the new form as the answer to 'degenerate' swing while the other, largely influenced by the revival of interest in the New Orleans form, denied that it had any merit whatsoever. The group of musicians who suffered most were the great individualists of the swing era who found themselves caught between the embattled partisans. Today, many years after the event, many of the revivalist followers in the U.S.A. are recording modernists quite happily and there is a tendency to suggest that the *furor* was about nothing of lasting importance. This is hardly so, for certain elements of the bop phase cannot be accepted by many critics and jazz fans who were not revivalist partisans either, and who are now putting forward a strong case for the mid-period musicians. However, this discussion is not

58

relevant in a study of Louis Armstrong except in so far as it is an important event in jazz history which had effects that were to cause the great trumpeter to face ill-conceived criticism from the musicians and admirers of the new school. Armstrong himself has been hostile to bop from the beginning, a reaction that is shared by many of his contemporaries and most musicians of the swing era. He recorded a skit on bop, using the melody of *The Whiffenpoof Song*, and has never retracted any of his acid comments on the new form. Many of the later criticisms concerning his stage behaviour have been made by followers of modern forms, although it is only fair to relate that musicians like Miles Davis and Dizzy Gillespie have maintained an attitude of praise for his actual playing throughout the years. Unlike some stars of the 'thirties, Armstrong has made no attempt to alter his style, and as far as his playing is concerned bop might not have happened.

In 1943 the magazine *Esquire* held the first of a series of jazz polls and Armstrong won both the trumpet and vocal categories. *Esquire* presented the first jazz concert ever held at the Metropolitan Opera House in New York City, in January 1944, and Armstrong had a featured role. It is unfortunate that the recording ban was still in force at the time, but some numbers have been issued on the private wartime V-Discs (which were for the use of the American armed forces only) and these have found their way into collectors' hands in some instances. The concert was an all-star affair and apart from Armstrong included

59

the late Art Tatum, Roy Eldridge, Jack Teagarden and Coleman Hawkins amongst the performers. The *Esquire* poll for 1945–46 saw Armstrong win the vocal section, while in 1947 he won both the trumpet and vocal categories. After this the magazine ceased to feature jazz to to any great extent.

In 1945 came the lifting of the recording ban and Armstrong was back in the studio by January 1945. A year elapsed before he recorded again, this time to make the first of many titles with Ella Fitzgerald. Both in personal appearances and on record the band behind him was becoming of less importance, for by now he was essentially the star performer and the orchestra's role was that of providing a suitable accompaniment. In any case, big bands were going through a very poor time as the result of many factors, one of which was the wartime-imposed entertainment tax which caused many club owners to fall back on smaller groups in the interest of economy. In 1946 Louis received an important acting part in the film *New Orleans*. This was a film that promised much but realized little, although there is some magnificent music in it by Armstrong and members of his pick-up group. The interesting aspect of this film from a musical viewpoint is that it resulted in Armstrong playing and recording with a small group once more, including the New Orleans trombone veteran Edward 'Kid' Ory who had just made a most successful comeback and had a role in the film. After the film was made Louis did not reorganize a big band, instead assembling a small unit which he has used, with personnel changes, down to the present day. This was the end of the big band era for Armstrong and apart from casual pick-up outfits in the recording studio he has not made any public appearances with one for well over a decade.

It has been said that jazz is a young man's music, but at the age of forty-six Armstrong was about to enter on the most hectic phase of his life and his fame was to grow throughout the next decade until his name became almost synonymous with jazz in the public mind. By now Joe Glaser had become his manager and Glaser, whatever his failings may be and some people insist that they are many, has handled Armstrong's business affairs astutely. He saw that the small group was both economically and artistically necessary to Armstrong if he was to continue to reach the widest possible public, and in 1946 he set about organizing one. The next ten years were to see Armstrong performing in many countries throughout the world and his fame grew equal to that of any concert virtuoso in the classical music field.

5

1947-59 — THE ALL STARS AND THE WORLD TRAVELLER

The story concerning the formation of the All Stars is told by Armstrong himself in the course of an interview with Sinclair Traill published in the book *Just Jazz* 1. He gives the credit to Glaser, as the following extract shows:

'Well the idea for the All Stars came from my manager, Joe Glaser. He knew that the days of big band bookings were fading out—that was in 1946—and so he formed the first All Stars to play at Billy Banks.

'Joe, he asked me what I'd like to do, would I like to come in, and I said it was up to him—to me it was just like the rabbit and the briar patch. We rehearsed two days and went in there. Joe picked them and sent them out to me in California where I was just finishin' the film *Song is Born*. Let me see, we had that trumpet man on piano, Dick Cary, Barney Bigard played clarinet, Big Sid Catlett was on drums, Jack Teagarden, trombone and Morty Cobb,

he played real good bass, came from out on the coast.

'No, I never pick my own bands—too many good musicians around, makes bad friends.'

Actually, some confusion exists as to exactly when the All Stars were formed. In his *Encyclopedia of Jazz* Leonard Feather claims that it was formed after the filming of *New Orleans* and not *A Song is Born*. The latter certainly would seem to be correct, for the former film was made in 1946 and the All Stars was not formed until a year later. We have the additional evidence of Jack Teagarden who says that Joe Glaser approached him during the memorable Town Hall concert in New York City of 24 April 1947 and asked him to be a member of the new group. The American magazine *Record Changer* carries a photographic supplement on the opening of the All Stars in Los Angeles in its October 1947 issue and the first recording date featuring the band took place on 16 October 1947. What is probable is that Glaser had the idea for the smaller group sometime in 1946 but it was not formed until the autumn of 1947. It is as well to mention the Town Hall concert before starting on the history of the All Stars.

An English collector, Peter Tanner, was present at the concert and mentioned it in the *Record Changer* of September 1947, in the following terms:

'My first introduction to the real jazz was at one of the last of this season's concerts at Town Hall where the featured soloists were to have been Louis Armstrong and Sidney Bechet. Unfortunately Sidney was taken ill on the day of the concert and was unable to appear, and so the whole concert had to be carried by Louis. Not that I had any complaints to make about this and Louis gave a truly magnificent performance, singing and playing at his very best. Starting off with *Cornet Chop Suey*, Louis went through most of the fine numbers that he recorded for Okeh in the old days, including a magnificent trumpet solo (with piano) version of *Dear Old Southland*. Louis was accompanied by Jack Teagarden, with whom he sang *Rockin' Chair*, Bobby Hackett, Peanuts Hucko, Bob Haggart, Dick Cary and Big Sid Catlett. These musicians simply played background to Louis and gave him intelligent and very adequate support.'

The concert was actually recorded and a few numbers have been generally released on the Victor and RCA labels, but it would be very interesting to discover if further selections are in the Victor vaults and, if so, why they remain unissued. One person who was particularly happy on the night of the concert was Jack Teagarden. The trombonist was just emerging from a period of extreme depression occasioned by the failure of his own big bands, and has related that he thought he played as well during the concert as at any time during his career. In retrospect, it seems very likely that the good reactions to the group which Armstrong used on this occasion may well have fortified Glaser in his view that a small band was the next step in promoting his charge.

The opening of the All Stars at Billy Bergs (not Billy

Banks as is quoted in the extract from *Just Jazz*) resulted in enthusiastic press notices and Glaser's perspicacity was proved. A concert at Boston on 30 November 1947 was recorded and later issued in long playing record form. The one change in the personnel which opened at Bergs was the replacement of Cobb by Arvell Shaw. In addition, the group has carried the controversial vocalist Velma Middleton from its inception. January 1948 saw Cary leaving to be replaced by none other than Earl Hines. In February 1948 the All Stars took part in a jazz festival in Nice and a number of recordings of broadcasts were made available, presumably without Armstrong's authority. Failing health caused Sidney Catlett to leave the band a few months before his death, and he was replaced by Cozy Cole in 1950.

There can be little doubt that the period of the All Stars, which brings one to the present day, has brought the greatest commercial success to Armstrong and has made him the best known jazz musician in the world. His life over the past decade has been one of constant travel. Before turning to the much debated questions of Armstrong's 'Uncle Tomism' and the repertoire which he has been using—questions which are relevant to his worth as a jazz musician at the present time—it is probably as well to bring the history of the All Stars up to the time of writing. In the summer of 1951 Teagarden was replaced by the ex-Jimmy Lunceford star, James 'Trummy' Young, and Young is still a member of the group. In 1955 Barney

Bigard was replaced by Edmond Hall, who was a member of the unit until 1958 when he left to free-lance. His place was taken by Michael 'Peanuts' Hucko. In 1953 Billy Kyle came in to take the place of Hines, whilst from May 1954 until the summer of 1958 Barrett Deems was the drummer who succeeded Cozy Cole. He in turn was replaced by Danny Barcelona. Arvell Shaw left the band in early 1958 and several bass players were tried, before Mort Herbert came in as a permanent member. Velma Middleton has been the permanent vocalist and entertainer for twelve years.

Foreign tours have played an increasing part in the itinerary of the All Stars and they toured in Europe in 1949 and again in 1952. In 1954 they appeared with great success in Japan and, in 1956, came the famous English appearances. After leaving England the band went on to France, Switzerland and other European countries, the tour culminating in a series of concerts in Ghana. This trip was the subject of an excellent documentary film, *The Satchmo Story*, directed by Ed Murrow, the well-known American television personality. In November 1956 Armstrong returned alone to play a single concert in aid of the Lord Mayor's Hungarian Relief Fund. The All Stars visited various South American countries in 1957 and, in March 1959, once more appeared in England and other European countries. Apart from the foreign trips the band is constantly moving from city to city in the United States, playing concerts at the jazz festivals, night club engagements, and various one-night appearances. Armstrong himself is a man nearly sixty years of age but this routine seems not to disturb him, and when I took part in a panel discussion at the Monterey, California Jazz Festival in October 1958 he was scathing about those musicians who refuse to tour.

Throughout these years Armstrong has recorded prolifically, both with his own group and with pick-up bands. His television and radio appearances are frequent and he has taken part in a number of films. Apart from the Ed Murrow documentary already mentioned, these latter have been very much in the stereotyped Hollywood convention and he has never appeared to advantage in them. Honours of all types have been heaped upon him, one of the most unusual being the citation presented to him by the House of Representatives at the State House in Boston in the early part of 1958. The citation read:

'Whereas, Louis Armstrong, the world's greatest trumpeter in the field of jazz music is about to celebrate his fiftieth year as a musician; and

'Whereas, Louis Armstrong has risen from humble origin to a pre-eminent position in the world of music and entertainment, and is a true exemplification of the strength of democratic principles and a shining example to all who aspire to greatness; and

'Whereas, Louis Armstrong by his artistry has through the universal language of music brought comfort, pleasure and understanding to people throughout the world, and is properly recognized as the outstanding ambassador of good will of our country; therefore be it

'Resolved, that the Massachusetts Senate extends its best wishes to Louis Armstrong and wishes him many years of health and happiness, so that he may continue to spread happiness for all people; and be it further

'Resolved, that copies of these resolutions be transmitted forthwith by the clerk of the Senate to Louis Armstrong.'

During the November 1956 concert a tribute was paid to Armstrong by Sir Laurence Olivier from the stage of the Royal Festival Hall. This concert was unusual in as far as Armstrong appeared with a small group of British musicians and also with the backing of the Royal Philharmonic Orchestra under the baton of Norman Del Mar. The results were curious to say the least. At one point Armstrong threw the orchestra into confusion by calling for an extra chorus which had not been pre-arranged. Mr. Del Mar was left conducting the air as the orchestra players scrambled to find the missing parts of the orchestration! This was not the first time that Louis had appeared with a symphony orchestra, for on the preceding June he had taken part in a concert at the Lewisohn Stadium in Chicago which featured a 'concert' arrangement of *St. Louis Blues*. On this occasion the conductor of the orchestra was Leonard Bernstein who has more than a casual acquaintance with jazz and was not likely to be disconcerted by any improvised additions to the score. The sequence when

Armstrong played the number was shown in the film *Satchmo the Great* and one of the most moving moments in the film comes when the camera is swung on W. C. Handy, the composer, who was in the audience.

It might be assumed that these last few years must be numbered amongst Armstrong's happiest, yet the situation has been marred by a number of attacks on his stage mannerisms and by an insidious campaign against him as an 'Uncle Tom'. It would be as well to consider something of the background of the campaign.

The bop revolution of the early forties has already been mentioned. What has sometimes been overlooked is that the movement was not only a musical revolt but a sociological one as well. The young musicians who took up bop so enthusiastically had none of the background of the pioneers of the form, and tolerance of older musicians and styles was almost completely absent as far as they were concerned. The 'modern' jazz movement grew up at a time when the American Negro was making considerable advances in the economic and social spheres, mainly as a result of the need for the co-operation of the Negro population during the Second World War. Naturally, the younger Negroes had no intention of allowing the position to deteriorate after the war was over and there grew up a demand for equality in all fields. This in itself is highly commendable and no rational person could be other than sympathetic to such ideals. However, with it there developed an attitude of resentment against the past which found expression in a curious hostility to any characteristics which could be typed as essentially Negroid. On its lowest level it could be seen in the rather pathetic advertisements in the Negro newspapers for hair-straighteners and skin bleaches, but in the world of the modern jazzmen the reaction took the form of rejecting the musical past and in an attempt to dismiss all earlier styles as the expression of an unhappy period which would be best forgotten. At the heart of the matter was a complete acceptance of the norms of the dominant white capitalist society with its success equated with material gains. Such a viewpoint differs very considerably from the outlook of racial minorities in most countries who are usually proud of their heritage and would not for one moment consider complete 'assimilation' as anything but another form of subjection. Along with this attitude went a declaration that bop was a music of social revolt, yet upon examination it is seen that such claims are bogus. In actual fact, there is much less revolt in modern jazz than in earlier forms, for a spurious bohemianism and turning away from one's audience is an indication of neurosis not revolt.

Time might well have taken care of the situation, but the position was complicated by the acceptance of the new music and the propagation of a theory of continual progress in jazz by many of the American journalists who wrote regularly for the mass circulation journals. It was somehow inevitable that Armstrong should have been singled out for the brunt of the attacks. As I have mentioned in an earlier chapter Armstrong comes from the era when musicians thought of themselves as entertainers and not as artists. It was perfectly natural that many of them should be excellent showmen who used comedy routines as part of their performance, and for two decades nobody had thought to question their right to do so. To the 'new' Negroes any suggestion of Southern Negro speech was tantamount to the worst sort of 'Uncle Tomming' (the definition of an Uncle Tom is a Negro who is obsequious to an exaggerated extent to white people) and, at the same time, the popularity of Armstrong shocked the more militant boppers. The 'progressive' critics mounted a campaign of hostility to Armstrong, his music and his personality that must be unparalleled in the history of jazz. It became routine to read that any concert by him was poor, that he clowned in an undignified manner on the stage and that, compared to the dignified modernists, he was a disgrace to his race. Curiously enough the same critics did not bother to hide their partisanship, as proved by their sympathetic writing, towards Charlie Parker, to give one example, who was involved in more disgraceful exhibitions in public than almost any other jazz performer. The fact is that Parker was a mentally sick man and I do not suggest that he should have been treated without sympathy, but the manner in which the same critics who would lean over backwards to present Parker in as agreeable a light as possible would seize every opportunity to belittle Armstrong showed that genuine concern for dignity was not involved in the polemics. In all, this was a disgraceful and shoddy campaign and people who know Armstrong well say that he was much hurt by it. Perhaps the height of the criticisms were reached during the Armstrong concert at the Newport Jazz Festival in 1957.

The organizers of the Newport Festival had decided to make the opening night a birthday tribute to Armstrong. It had been claimed that he was to present a new programme and had agreed to certain other musicians making guest appearances with him. Exactly what did happen on that night it is impossible to decide, but there is no doubt that by the time Armstrong took the stage he was a very angry man. What should have been a happy occasion turned out to be something of a fiasco and the concert was abruptly concluded in an atmosphere of rancour. One of the musicians who was to have played with Armstrong on that occasion was Jack Teagarden, and when he was touring England a few months later he told me that Armstrong had been blamed unfairly in his opinion and that the real fault lay with the Newport Festival organizers. It does seem certain that there had been a considerable amount of provocation on the night of the concert and that by the time that the great trumpeter took the stage he had been goaded beyond the point of reasonableness. One story has it that two well-known critics had approached him and demanded that he present a new programme in a manner to which he took strong exception. In one way

72

and another this unhappy episode reflects little credit on those who were dealing with the presentation of the programme.

The demand that Armstrong should speak out on social and racial matters is, in any case, a curious one. If the truth be told there have been very few jazz musicians who have cared to brand themselves as outspoken social critics and for all the sound and fury from the modernist camp these performers have not been noticeably less reticent in the matter. Many of the modernists have turned to Mohammedanism because of its racial tolerance but they have displayed no public militancy in social matters or, if they have, it has surprisingly not been reported. In September 1957 Armstrong dropped a bombshell amongst his critics. It was the period of Governor Faubus's defiance of the Supreme Court on the matter of racial integration, and in an angry interview Armstrong denounced President Eisenhower as 'two-faced', and said that he was permitting Faubus to 'run the country'. He cancelled his proposed tour of Russia for the State Department, 'because the way they are treating my people in the south, the government can go to hell'. This is probably the most widely publicized and outspoken comment on racial matters that a public entertainer has ever made, but the reaction of the critics who had been maligning Armstrong has been as despicable as their former attacks. Not one publicly associated himself with Armstrong's remarks and in spite of their much boasted liberalism, the modernist musicians were not exactly headlong in their rush to support him. From this time the campaign seems to have died down and one hopes that the motives of those conducting it have been sufficiently discredited. The fact that anyone who has met Armstrong could really consider him an 'Uncle Tom', as some critics maintained, is a sign of singular stupidity or sheer wilful antagonism.

Although it is an entirely different matter the critics who were involved in the 'Uncle Tom' campaign also took every opportunity to point out that the repertoire of Armstrong's concerts consisted of the same group of numbers and blasted Velma Middleton's antics on the stage. The charge of sameness of repertoire is partly justified, but Armstrong himself spoke on the subject in his interview with Sinclair Traill in *Just Jazz* 1. His comments are worth quoting:

'Lot of people say why don't we play more new tunes each night? Well y' know it's a real consolation always gettin' that same note—just hittin' it right. The public can get to know you better by them old tunes than by anything new. So, like Heifetz and Marian Anderson, we play the same tunes; every time they play the same solo they get the applause—so do we.'

The comparison with performers in another field might be considered ingenuousness but one has to remember that Armstrong still thinks of himself primarily as an entertainer, and that the jazz fans as such must now form a very slight segment of his audience. Armstrong is also in a somewhat similar position to the late Art Tatum in as far as he considers that he has, over the years, evolved set solos that he is incapable of bettering. John McLellan has dealt with this point ably in the *Boston Traveler* of 29 July 1958:

'Louis is not trying to prove how fast he can run the chord changes of a tune. Nor how many choruses of variations he can string together. If, over a period of time, he has composed through improvisation a perfect solo—a solo with a rhythmic structure that swings, and a melodic structure that expresses beauty—why try to change it? And Louis plays plenty of perfect solos.'

In actual fact if one has the opportunity of hearing Armstrong on succeeding nights it is sometimes surprising to note just how much he does alter his solo within a pre-established framework. A comparison of versions of numbers that he has recorded more than once in the last few years will show many variations. I feel that the problem is confused by the lingering belief of many fans that a true jazz performance should be completely improvised. The history of the music from the time of Oliver and Jelly Roll Morton gives the lie to this reasoning. I must admit, in all honesty, that I would personally prefer to hear some new numbers at Armstrong's public performances, but a wish of this nature should not blind one to the quality of the music that one hears. The antics of Velma Middleton on the stage are also not greatly to my liking and I have no great respect for her as a vocalist, but one accepts her as part of the show and it is essential lize that a show is what it is in Armstrong's own

...day after a half century of playing Armstrong is as dedicated a performer as he ever was. He takes considerable care of his health—his belief in a particular laxative must be known to all who have met him!—and drinks moderately and is only an occasional smoker. He has the attitude of a professional to his job and is not unaware of his own worth, although the latter attitude is an acceptance of reality rather than egotism. Armstrong the man is a blend of genuine humility and strength of character. He is also extremely generous to fellow musicians who have fallen on difficult times, but his charity is done unobtrusively. I found that all the musicians who came up in the 'twenties and early 'thirties idolized Armstrong both as a musician and man and in a curious sort of way they felt that his success was a vindication of their own attitude and style. Armstrong the public performer is one thing but the man as a private individual is probably only known to a few intimates. He has a considerable perspicacity in summing up a man's character and some of the musicians I met in New York reported some devastating comments on well-known critics and agents that he had made.

As a performer in 1959 I am convinced that Armstrong remains the greatest trumpeter in jazz and, indeed, the greatest creative genius in the history of the music. His records in the last decade have been of a very variable quality, but the special occasion can still bring out the

76

greatness in him. He has the habit of producing records that still all criticism after a succession of routine performances. The famous 'Louis Armstrong Plays W. C. Handy' LP of 1955 must rate amongst his greatest releases and there are many quite magnificent tracks in the four-volume set that he recorded during 1956–57 for Decca (released in England on the Brunswick label). This took the form of a musical autobiography with Armstrong himself commenting on the numbers which started with a group that he had first played with the King Oliver band. It is interesting to note that certain titles are superior to the original performances, notably *King of the Zulus*, *Georgia On My Mind* and *Lazy River*. The American writer Martin Williams summarized his reactions to some of these tracks in a review of the set in the December 1958 *Jazz Review*, and his remarks are so apt that I am quoting them here:

'It is all very well to talk about Armstrong's rhythmic conception, about his transformations of banal melodies, about the superb imagination of an harmonic variation like that in the 1938 *I Can't Give You Anything But Love*, about "the first great jazz soloist." It is also all very well to say that this *King of the Zulus* is not like the first. It happens to be better. On it, and on the other titles for which I have reserved comment, Armstrong is astonishing, and astonishing because he plays with such great power, authority, sureness, firmness, commanding presence as to be beyond style, beyond category, almost (as they say of

Beethoven's last quartets) beyond music. When he plays the trumpet this way, all considerations of "schools", most other jazzmen, most other musicians simply drop away as we listen. The show biz personality act, the coasting, the forced jokes and sometimes forced geniality, the perpetual emotional content of much of Armstrong's music past and present (that of a marvellously exuberant but complex child)—all these drop away, and we are hearing a surpassing artist create for us—each of us— a surpassing art.'

Mr. Williams correctly summarized the Armstrong of today. Quite often his shows are routine, although it is seldom that he does not play something of worth, and now and then the more commercial records sound somewhat forced. If, at the age of fifty-nine, Armstrong sometimes decides to take it easy who is there to blame him? Although strongly expressed, his remarks that 'some of them modern trumpeters couldn't carry out my routine, why man, they would be carried away on stretchers!' has the ring of truth about it. Armstrong has been playing so superbly for so many years that his lapses are understandable. The dawning of an adult appreciation of jazz, as of any art form, begins when one realizes that one's idols have their off-days and their moments of aberration. The truly astonishing factor in Armstrong's career is that out of the hundreds of records that he has made there are so very few that are entirely without interest. If he now decides to conserve some of the creativity for the special event or recording it seems an entirely logical decision, yet the fact remains that as he approaches sixty years of age he can still show the same flashes of genius as he did when he was in his twenties.

Those of us who have grown up with jazz for any length of time have rather developed the attitude of acceptance where Armstrong is concerned. It is to be presumed that sometime during the next decade he will retire from music and then the full force of what we have lost will become apparent. It will be a sad day when Armstrong plays no more, even though we do have the wonderful legacy of his records, and something will have gone from jazz that is irreplaceable. Armstrong has been with jazz almost from the beginning and as it grew so did he. The entertainment world in which he has moved is a cynical, dishonest one, but he was much too big to be influenced by it. He remains one of the very few artists who has added something worthwhile to the lives of others and before his achievements the occasional failures seem unimportant. It would be fitting to let a musician who has played with him relate his feelings on Armstrong's importance, and I am concluding with the words, quoted in the 22 January 1959 issue of *Down Beat*, of one of the most thoughtful and literate musicians in jazz. In the course of an interview with Tom Scanlan, Teddy Wilson had the following to say about Armstrong:

'I think Louis is the greatest jazz musician that's ever been. He had a combination of all the factors that makes

a good musician. He had balance . . . this most of all.
Tone. Harmonic sense. Excitement. Technical skill.
Originality. Every musician, no matter how good, usually
has something out of balance, be it tone, too much imi-
tativeness, or whatever. But in Armstrong everything
was in balance. He had no weak point. Of course, I am
speaking in terms of the general idiom of his day. Trumpet
playing is quite different today than it was then.

'I don't think there has been a musician since Armstrong
who has had all the factors in balance, all the factors
equally developed. Such a balance was the essential thing
about Beethoven, I think, and Armstrong, like Beethoven,
had this high development of balance. Lyricism. Delicacy.
Emotional outburst. Rhythm. Complete mastery of his
horn.'

SELECTED DISCOGRAPHY

RECOMMENDED RECORDS BY OR FEATURING
LOUIS ARMSTRONG

1923–24 *with* King Oliver's Creole Jazz Band

> *Snake Rag, Mabel's Dream, Room Rent Blues,*
> *Dippermouth Blues, I Ain't Gonna Tell Nobody,*
> *Working Man's Blues, High Society, Sweet Baby*
> *Doll, Sobbin' Blues, London Cafe Blues, My Sweet*
> *Lovin' Man, Camp Meeting Blues*
>
> Epic LN–3208

> *Chimes Blues, Just Gone, Canal Street Blues,*
> *Mandy Lee Blues, Weather Bird Rag, Dipper*
> *Mouth Blues, Froggie Moore, Snake Rag, Mabel's*
> *Dream, Southern Stomps, Riverside Blues,*
>
> Riverside RLP12–122

1923–25 *with* King Oliver's Creole Jazz Band, Fletcher
Henderson's Orchestra, Red Onion Jazz Babies,
Ma Rainey, Trixie Smith

> *Alligator Hop, Krooked Blues, I'm Going Away*
> *To Wear You Off My Mind, Mandy Make Up Your*
> *Mind, Jelly Bean Blues, Countin' The Blues, Ter-*
> *rible Blues, Santa Claus Blues, Of All The Wrongs*
> *You've Done To Me, Nobody Knows The Way I*

81

Feel This Morning, Cake Walking Babies From Home, Railroad Blues

Riverside RLP12–101

1924–25 *with* Bessie Smith

St. Louis Blues, I Ain't Gonna Play No Second Fiddle, You've Been A Good Old Wagon, Sobbin' Hearted Blues, Reckless Blues, Careless Love Blues, Cold In Hand Blues

included in Columbia CL–855

1925–27 Hot Five

Muskrat Ramble, Heebie Jeebies, Gut Bucket Blues, Skid-Dat-De-Dat, Yes! I'm In The Barrel, Cornet Chop Suey, Struttin' With Some Barbecue, I'm Not Rough, The Last Time, Got No Blues, Hotter Than That, Ory's Creole Trombone

Columbia CL–851

1925–27 *with* Erskine Tate's Vendome Orchestra, Red Onion Jazz Babies, Johnny Dodds, Lil's Hot Shots

Static Strut, Stomp Off Let's Go, Terrible Blues, Santa Claus Blues, Wild Man Blues, Melancholy, Georgia Bo Bo, Drop That Sack

Brunswick BL–58004 (now deleted)

1927 Hot Seven

Potato Head Blues, Wild Man Blues, S.O.L. Blues, Gully Low Blues, Melancholy Blues, Weary Blues, Twelfth Street Rag, Willie The Weeper, Keyhole Blues, That's When I'll Come Back To You, Alligator Crawl, Chicago Breakdown

Columbia CL–852

82

1928   Savoy Ballroom Five

Basin Street Blues, Weather Bird, No, Papa, No,
Muggles, St. James Infirmary, Tight Like This,
West End Blues, Skip The Gutter, Two Deuces,
Sugar Foot Strut, Squeeze Me, Don't Jive Me
                              Columbia CL–853

1929–31 *with* Orchestras under actual leadership of Les
        Hite, Carroll Dickerson, Leon Herriford and Luis
        Russell

Knockin' A Jug, Body And Soul, Stardust (two
takes), *Black And Blue, I Can't Give You Any-*
thing But Love, Lazy River, Dear Old Southland,
If I Could Be With You, I'm Confessin', I'm A
Ding Dong Daddy, Shine
                              Columbia CL–854

1937–39 *with* Orchestras under the actual leadership of
        Jimmy Dorsey and Luis Russell

When The Saints Go Marching In, Bye And Bye,
West End Blues, Mahogany Hall Stomp, Dipper-
mouth Blues, Save It Pretty Mama, You Rascal
You, When It's Sleepy Time Down South, Hear
Me Talkin' To Ya, Savoy Blues, Our Monday Date,
Wolverine Blues
                              Decca DL–8284

1935–41 *with* Orchestra directed by Luis Russell

Shadrack, Jeepers Creepers, Old Man Mose, Shoe
Shine Boy, Brother Bill, Now Do You Call That
A Buddy, On The Sunny Side Of The Street, Con-
fessin', Ain't Misbehavin', I Can't Give You Any-

83

thing But Love, Sweethearts On Parade, Baby Won't You Please Come Home

Decca DL–8327

1940   *with* pick-up group including Sidney Bechet

2.19 Blues, Perdido Street Blues, Coal Cart Blues, Down In Honky Tonk Town

included in Decca DL–8283

1947   All-Star Groups, Esquire Award Winners

Rockin' Chair, Ain't Misbehavin', Back O'Town Blues, Long, Long Journey, Mahogany Hall Stomp, Pennies From Heaven, St. James Infirmary, Save It Pretty Mama, Some Day, Sugar, Snafu

Victor LPM–1443

1950   All Stars

Panama, New Orleans Function, Flee As A Bird, Oh, Didn't He Ramble, Struttin' With Some Barbecue, Basin Street Blues, My Bucket's Got A Hole In It, Bugle Call Rag

Decca DL–8329

1954   All Stars—'Play W. C. Handy'

St. Louis Blues, Yellow Dog Blues, Loveless Love, Aunt Hagar's Blues, Long Gone, Memphis Blues, Beale Street Blues, Ole Miss, Chantez Les Bas, Hesitating Blues, Atlanta Blues

Columbia CL–591

1956   All Stars and Lewisohn Stadium Symphony Orchestra (valuable as a documentary)

When It's Sleepy Time Down South, Indiana,

*Interview In Paris With Edward R. Murrow, Flee
As A Bird To The Mountain, Oh Didn't He Ram-
ble, Mack The Knife, Mahogany Hall Stomp, All
For You, Louis, Black And Blue, St. Louis Blues*
Columbia CL–1077

1956–57 All Stars and studio group directed by Sy Oliver
(This is a musical autobiography re-creating many
of Armstrong's great hits of the period 1923–33,
with spoken comments by Armstrong)

*Dippermouth Blues, Canal Street Blues, High
Society, Of All The Wrongs You've Done To Me,
Everybody Loves My Baby, Mandy, Make Up
Your Mind, Them There Eyes, Lazy River, Georgia
On My Mind, That's My Home, Hobo, You Can't
Ride This Train, On The Sunny Side Of The Street*

*See See Rider, Reckless Blues, Court House Blues,
Trouble In Mind, New Orleans Function, Gut
Bucket Blues, If I Could Be With You One Hour,
Body and Soul, Memories Of You, You Rascal You,
When It's Sleepy Time Down South, I Surrender
Dear*

*Cornet Chop Suey, Heebie Jeebies, Georgia Grind,
Muskrat Ramble, King of the Zulus, Snag It, Some
Of These Days, When You're Smiling, Song of
The Islands, I Can't Believe That You're In Love
With Me, Dear Old Southland, Exactly Like You*

*Wild Man Blues, Potato Head Blues, Weary Blues,
Gully Low Blues, Struttin' With Some Barbecue,
Hotter Than That, Two Deuces, My Monday Date,
Basin Street Blues, Knockin' A Jug, I Can't Give
You Anything But Love, Mahogany Hall Stomp*
Decca DL–8604–7

(These four 12″ LPs available only as a set number DXM–155)

1957　*with* Ella Fitzgerald and Oscar Peterson Group

Don't Be That Way, Makin' Whoopee, They All Laughed, Comes Love, Autumn In New York, Let's Do It, Stompin' At The Savoy, I Won't Dance, Gee, Baby Ain't I Good To You

Verve MGV–4017

Note: All records listed, apart from the ten-inch deleted LP Brunswick BL–58004, are twelve-inch long playing items. The only period not adequately represented on record is 1932–33, but RCA Victor may possibly issue a selection of titles in the future.